I0474689

LEARN HOW TO AUTOMATE YOUR BUSINESS PROFESSIONALLY

HOW TO DELEGATE TASKS TO FREELANCERS, DISCOVER THE POWER OF OUTSOURCING

Jorge O. Chiesa

Table of Contents

INTRODUCTION

Entrepreneurs and small business owners often work longer hours than they need because they try to handle all aspects of their business on their own. However, this can quickly lead to burnout and failure. In business, results matter, and your goal is to produce the best results. The best way to do this is to form a team of experts who can help you succeed.

Unfortunately, many companies cannot manage all of their business processes due to the limitations of their employees. As the owner and leader of your business, it is your job to focus on the strengths of your organization.

If you are your company's developer or marketing expert, it is very likely that you lack knowledge of accounting or customer service. This is why outsourcing has become a fast-growing alternative for many small business owners.

Outsourcing is the assignment of various business processes to people and expert companies. These professionals handle the business tasks that you have identified as needs. Outsourcing the non-strategic operations of your business allows you to focus on the parts of your business that are most important to you.

Virtual outsourcing is a fast-growing trend in which organizations of all sizes outsource business processes to professionals around the world. This is known as self-employment and is the preferred method for small and medium businesses.

Outsourcing gained its popularity in the mid-1980s and has grown steadily ever since. It was first used by small and new businesses struggling to survive in a competitive market.

Today, companies of all sizes have adopted outsourcing to help them complete various business processes. The most common businesses that take advantage of outsourcing are Internet-based, and many companies rely solely on the self-employed to run their businesses.

With the growing popularity and recognition that outsourcing is a viable business alternative for today's businesses, it is now possible for anyone to start and run a business without having to worry about finding cheap office space or strict government regulations and taxes.

Outsourcing is extremely beneficial for business owners because they are given the opportunity to concentrate on growing their business. Most outsourced tasks are performed by part-time freelancers, allowing you to avoid having to employ full-time staff.

This will allow you to save on numerous benefits such as health insurance and paid vacations, giving you the opportunity to reinvest the money saved in your business.

You can hire almost any type of professional to work as a virtual employee. This includes designers, accountants, writers, programmers, IT professionals, salespeople and many more. All you need is a computer and the Internet to search, hire, communicate and work with virtual professionals from all over the world.

There are several advantages associated with outsourcing certain business processes, especially when it is a well-managed process. However, there are times when outsourcing can be counterproductive and lead to business losses.

This is especially true when contracts and project management resources are scarce.

CHAPTER I
EXTERNALIZATION

One of the most important things you have to consider before talking about the advantages of outsourcing is that it may not be a great option if you are only interested in making massive profits.

You will need to evaluate whether outsourcing will be a viable option for you or whether you need to look for other alternatives to complete the task.

The United States and India are among the top outsourcing countries in the world. Here are some of the advantages your business can gain by outsourcing some of its business processes.

Advantages for your business

One of the most significant advantages

of outsourcing your business tasks is that it allows you to start with little, unlike hiring employees, which is a substantial investment. Starting small becomes an essential way to perfect your delegation skills.

Outsourcing allows you to delegate mundane tasks that slowly begin to consume your valuable time. If you hire employees to complete these tasks, you could end up costing more than it's worth.

Having freelancers and remote workers can help free up your time so you can concentrate on the essentials of running your business. Outsourcing allows you to manage your business from anywhere in the world, as long as you have access to the Internet.

It gives you the opportunity to travel, visit friends and spend long weekends out of town without losing the ability to complete essential business projects. When you outsource, you don't have to have an office. This is a considerable advantage of outsourcing.

Outsourcing allows you to quickly access skills for anything you need. You don't have to spend money or time training new employees and you can build a network of freelancers, allowing you to perform any task quickly and easily.

Since you can hire people who love to perform the tasks you hate, outsourcing can help reduce your stress. It can also reduce stress when you lose an employee. Having to go through the hiring process takes a lot of time, which makes your business difficult every time you have to replace an employee who has left the company. Freelancers are much easier to replace.

Outsourcing is also a great way to complete temporary or seasonal tasks. You can bring them in for a short period of time without having to deal with hiring, training, and eventually letting them go when the project is finished.

If you are starting your business, outsourcing is a great way to get your business up and running. It allows you to pay for specific tasks instead of spending your time and money hiring employees.

Outsourcing your business processes can also save you a ton of money. Not only can you pay international fees, unlike your country's fees, but you don't have to worry about health insurance, vacation or sick pay, or any other type of costs that are normally associated with running a business.

Advantages for the customer

Outsourcing not only provides benefits for your company, but is also advantageous for your customers. In most cases, when you outsource your business processes, this leads to a lower cost of producing the goods and services you offer.

When you spend less on production, you can pass those savings on to the consumer through lower prices on finished products.

Provides Employment Opportunities

One of the most substantial advantages of outsourcing is the global employment opportunities it offers. Suppose a single company outsources several business processes to a few hundred workers located around the world, then thousands of companies that outsource work could result in millions of people getting jobs.

Employment is one of the most critical issues facing today's world leaders. By outsourcing its business processes to countries with high unemployment rates, it can help reduce the number of unemployed people, which translates into better economic conditions for people around the world.

Disadvantages of subcontracting

Unfortunately, as with any business task, outsourcing can have its drawbacks. There will be cases where your favorite freelance is not available to help you with an urgent task. Fortunately, there are ways to avoid this problem.

The best option is to have three or more freelancers you can turn to for each area of your business you want to outsource. While finding enough talented freelancers to work with can be time consuming and stressful, especially when working with tight deadlines, proper planning and networking, you can limit this problem.

You may also have to overcome a language barrier, depending on where you are looking to outsource. This can cause misunderstandings that could be detrimental to the success of your business.

To avoid this, you should make sure that you are providing detailed written instructions to freelancers along with screenshots or an instructional video to ensure that everything is 100 percent clear.

Remote workers have to be self-motivated and have a great deal of self-discipline, in addition to being extremely organized. Since you won't be there to motivate them personally, you have to find self-employed workers who possess these skills. This can sometimes be difficult to find.

Outsourcing requires you to continually increase your skills as a supervisor so that you can manage your freelancers. This does not mean that you should micro-manage them. There is a considerable difference between micro-management and management.

You should also expect to spend some time writing emails, making calls and completing other tasks that are associated with outsourcing. The general rule is that you should spend 20 percent of your time completing 100 percent of the functions you are outsourcing.

How to know when to outsource

This will depend entirely on the task you wish to delegate and the stage of your business. If you are starting a new business, then outsourcing is your best option about 99 percent of the time.

You will only need to hire an employee once you reach a certain stage of your business. Even then, you may decide that outsourcing is best.

CHAPTER II
IDENTIFYING YOUR NEEDS

The business outsourcing process starts with the knowledge that you have a need, sometimes even before you know it. You may think you don't need help, or that you can't bear the idea of paying someone else to do the work you can do yourself.

However, it is essential to think about the long-term success of your business. You need to admit that you will need help from time to time and start implementing preventive measures.

The challenge is to decide which tasks to keep at home and which to outsource. You want to outsource any business process that is not critical to your company's day-to-day operations.

If you have a simple business model, this will be easy to achieve. If your business has a more complex model, this process will require more time.

The first thing you need to do is to differentiate the business process into strategic or core processes and non-strategic or support processes.

It is crucial that you make the right decision now.

To identify the most suitable business processes for outsourcing, it is necessary to list all the processes and tasks that are completed in the course of the business. Then create a two-column table and rank each task according to its strategic importance.

One column should be labeled as "strategically important" and the other as "strategically unimportant. The tasks that you want to place in the "strategically important" column are those that are related to your business' competitive advantage.

These are tasks that may require giving access to confidential information that is important to complete these tasks. If you decide to outsource any of these tasks, you may want the freelancer to sign a Confidentiality Agreement or NDA. T

The questions placed in the "strategically unimportant" column are those that do not impact your company's competitive advantage and those that do not require an NDA signature.

Everyday tasks to consider outsourcing

In today's competitive business world, almost any business process can be outsourced. Here is a list of some of the more common tasks you should consider outsourcing.

Administrative Tasks

You can outsource many of the administrative tasks of your business to talented freelancers. When you're starting your business, these are the tasks you want to outsource quickly so you can start developing your delegation skills and start focusing on the most critical aspects of your business.

1) Virtual Assistant

When you don't have to worry about appointments, car services, reservations, deliveries, blog management and social media presence, you suddenly have a lot of free time to focus on more critical aspects of managing your business. Outsourcing these tasks to a virtual assistant will free up a considerable amount of time.

2) Email

One of the most time-consuming things you will have to do as a business owner is manage your email. When outsourcing email management, it should include email filtering, creating databases, sending invitations to events, managing calendars, and scheduling appointments.

3) Accounting

Accounting is one of the tasks that many new business owners try to tackle, only to end up in financial trouble. Accounting requires a lot of educational experience, as well as the time to keep up with constantly changing tax codes. The daily accounting tasks that most businesses need are time-consuming, making it almost impossible for business owners to devote enough time to growing their business. Outsourcing this task will not only save you time, but also money.

4) Data Entry

Having all your company's information easily organized, accessible and easy to share will help increase your productivity. However, this task requires a lot of time. Freelance data entry workers can not only manage their files, but they can also keep their online presence up to date, updating any information that changes over time.

5) Research

Often, as you grow your business, you need to conduct research. This may include finding new marketing strategies or writing a book. These tasks will require a ton of research. Unfortunately, research can consume your valuable time. You should consider outsourcing this task to work on more productive projects.

6) Project Management

When you start hiring more freelancers and have many outsourcing tasks running, it will take you a long time to manage and pay everyone. To help free up your time, you can hire a project manager to handle the task. This will be very useful because they will interact with all the freelancers, leaving you the only task of interacting with the project manager.

Content Creation

These next tasks will fall under the category of content creation. If you are a writer yourself, you can decide to handle these tasks on your own, while outsourcing programming and graphic design tasks to a group of independent professionals.

7) Social Networks

Your social media presence can present a great opportunity to generate money for your business, which can grow your brand identity. With the different social media platforms that are available, you have the opportunity to interact with thousands of potential new customers.

However, creating and publishing quality content on a daily basis can be time-consuming. Outsourcing your social media marketing to a company or individual experience is a great way to interact with your potential customers on a daily basis without having to spend your time doing it yourself.

8) Article Writing

With the popularity of blogs, the demand for high-quality articles loaded with valuable information has increased dramatically in recent years. The need for high quality content is endless and includes virtually any topic you can imagine. Visitors who should be provided with real information.

This is something Google knows well and has continually improved its indexing methods to ensure that valuable content is ranked higher on its search engine. Because demand is so high in this area, you should consider outsourcing this task in order to take advantage of this revenue stream.

9) Editing

Editing is an integral part of writing. It is a much sought-after and often underestimated skill. Editing is not simply the process of checking for spelling and grammatical errors, it is a whole process designed to make the text easier to read.

This can be accomplished through content editing, text editing and proofreading. It is essential that you be specific about the types of edits you need to complete when speaking with an independent professional, as simple proofreading is a much cheaper task than full editions.

10) eBooks and Physical Books

A popular method for sharing valuable information is eBooks. With the popularity of iBook, Nook, and Kindle, eBooks have become a compelling way to market your business.

Experts can write books that not only market your business, but also provide you with substantial benefits. This can be the most cost-effective form of outsourcing within the content writing category.

11) Business Plans

An essential part of any business is the business plan. However, nearly 70 percent of new business owners have not developed a business plan before opening their doors.

This could explain why the business failure rate is so high. If you're not sure where to start or don't want to sit down and write your business plan, this is where outsourcing can help.

Freelancers with experience in writing business plans can take on the task and create a plan for success that will help you stay on the right track.

12) Copy of sales

An essential aspect of your long-term success is having your sales copy in perfect shape. However, this can be an expensive and time-consuming task. You may have already tried to write your own sales letter or promotional descriptions, only to be disappointed when you can't see an increase in your sales.

Writing sales texts is a particular skill that not everyone possesses. Sales copywriting experts know how to incorporate label lines, provocative headlines, well-defined lists, and a compelling call to action. Sales copywriting is not limited to written descriptions, but can also include advertising scripts and presentations.

13) Email Marketing

Email marketing campaigns are extremely powerful for attracting new customers and increasing sales. Email marketing professionals are experts at creating email marketing campaigns that produce results. They will write the email, set up an automatic response system and target specific consumers.

Programming and Multimedia

As with content creation, if your company specializes in programming and multimedia, you may want to consider performing these tasks on your own and outsourcing content production.

14) Website Design

In today's competitive marketplace, if your business does not have a website, you are going to be at a considerable disadvantage. Most small business owners know this, which does not surprise them that web design has so much demand.

Website design is one of the most outsourced tasks in the world. Websites are something every business needs, but only a handful of select individuals have the skills to make them a reality.

15) Kindle Book Submissions

One of the best ways to promote your eBook is to send it to several websites that offer book reviews and have a solid base of followers. However, sending your book to more than 50 sites can be time-consuming. Outsourcing this task will save you a significant amount of time.

16) Google AdWords Campaigns

You can become a millionaire if you can develop a successful AdWords campaign. However, learning the process is difficult and can result in a considerable waste of time and money if you are not an expert on Google. AdWords. Outsourcing this task to a certified Google AdWords professional expert is highly recommended.

17) Search Engine Optimization (SEO)

SEO requires a particular skill set. No one knows the exact code that Google uses to index websites, so SEO specialists tend to test different variables. This gives them a unique advantage over others who don't fully understand the complexities of SEO. You can hire freelancers to place banners, create SEO-friendly blogs, and manage your pay-per-click campaigns to make sure you get the highest conversion rate.

18) Transcription Services

A great way to attract your readers and potential customers is to have video and audio files at your disposal. One way to increase the amount of content you add to your site is to hire a transcriptionist to write the information that appears in the video or audio file, word for word. This will provide you with a ton of articles to use on your website.

19) Voiceovers

People love audio content. It's very attractive and full of valuable information. Whether it's accompanied by a video or an audiobook, it's essential that it sounds professional and is of high quality. That's why it's best to hire a professional with the right equipment for the purpose and save a ton of time.

20) Graphic Design

Graphic design is another skill that is in high demand. Your company uses graphics for logos, brands, presentations, product descriptions and even videos.

Unless graphic design is in your skill set, it is highly recommended that you outsource this work.

21) Videos

Studies have determined that videos are 600 percent more appealing than plain text. They are simply too valuable for your business to do without. The videos your business may need include product demonstrations, reviews and even entertainment.

Great videos will sell, while poor videos have the potential to scare their customers. It is essential to work with professionals who can improve, edit and shoot videos so that they are 100 percent ready to be posted online.

22) Animation

Another type of video that you can use in your business are animated whiteboard videos. They can explain your business or service in an attractive and entertaining way and are quite handsome. They are one of the best tools to turn visitors into paying customers.

Combine these animation videos with a professional voice-over and you will have created a sales machine. However, creating such videos can take a long time if you are not an expert in the field.

23) Mobile Applications

Developing a mobile application for your business is one of the few real opportunities that can lead you to become a millionaire. Mobile applications are in extremely high demand right now, and getting an idea for a developed application can be enormously profitable. If you don't have the skills to build a mobile application, outsource the task, like most other Internet millionaires.

24) Formatting and Conversion

Although you can upload a simple Word document to Amazon, they don't usually convert very well. Many people and businesses need experts who can format and convert books so that they look and work perfectly on any device. If you don't have the experience to do this yourself, find a professional to complete the conversion for you.

Things to keep in mind before delegating tasks

Before you begin your search for talented independent professionals to outsource your business processes, there are a few things to keep in mind.

When it comes to freelancers, you need to pay close attention to your homeland. Although this will not matter for some tasks such as data entry and accounting, it could pose a potential problem when outsourcing writing tasks.

Beware of new contractors. Although there is nothing wrong with occasionally hiring someone who is looking to establish feedback, you will want to talk to them directly before doing so. If they're not willing to talk to you, don't hire them.

Pay attention to a freelancer's work history when making your decision. Some of the factors you'll want to consider include customer comments, comments, and their most recent work.

Consider interviewing potential candidates before offering them the job. You can conduct an oral interview or use emails or Skype to send messages to potential candidates. Ask them difficult questions and pay close attention to how they respond.

Start with a trial job. Give selected candidates a small task to do before hiring them. This will allow you to test your skill level. Keep in mind that you will have to pay them for the work they do, but starting with a small task is best to reduce the risk.

CHAPTER III
FINDING WORKERS

Now that you've determined which business processes you want to outsource, it's time to begin the process of finding qualified outsourcers. This can be a cumbersome task in itself if you don't know where to start.

There are hundreds of sites on the Internet where you can start your search for freelancers. However, it is important to understand that not all outsourcing organizations are created equal.

To help you find the best freelancers on the easiest to use platforms, we have compiled the following list of online companies that are designed to help individuals and companies find talented professionals to help them with their business processes.

Popular sites for hiring freelancers:

Upwork (www.upwork.com)

This is one of the most popular freelance sites on the Internet and is a great place to find talented freelancers. Getting started on the site is simple.

The easiest way to do the job is to divide the process into three phases:

1) Before hiring

2) Recruitment

3) Do the work.

Before hiring, you must make sure to fill in your company name, slogan, website description and address, and upload your company logo. Then add and verify your payment method. This is important because you can't hire freelancers without it. Then post the work and choose between hourly or fixed price.

Fiverr (www.fiverr.com)

You can hire practically any freelance for any job imaginable at Fiverr. Concerts start at $5, making it a great place to learn the basics of outsourcing. The site allows you to gain experience in choosing a freelancer, hiring them and providing feedback.

Fiverr works on what they call concerts. A concert usually costs only $5. However, you can rarely get quality work for that small amount of money. There are concert extras that are offered by more experienced vendors, giving you a higher quality job at a fairly reasonable price.

Freelancer.com (www.freelancer.com)

Freelancer.com has over a million freelancers to choose from and is a great place to find affordable rates. However, it is not as powerful as Upwork, so you should carefully select your candidates.

Freelancer gives you easy access to

graphic designers, writers, programmers and video editors. It serves as a great place to establish a great list of freelancers for all categories.

Guru (www.guru.com)

Guru is not as big as Upwork, but it is growing at an amazing rate. On the site you can find freelancers of all categories. One of the unique features of Guru is the way you list your project.

Based on the description you provide; Guru will send you a list of the best candidates for your listing. This gives you the power to choose which candidates you want to invite to apply for your job.

Guru is a great place for you to build your list of freelancers and is one of the most efficient outsourcing sites on the Internet.

99 Designs (www.99designs.com)

99 Designs is a different type of outsourcing site than the sites listed

above. It is what is known as a marketplace of design contests. To find freelancers, you need to publish a description of your project; then, freelancers will submit entries based on your description.

Then you can choose your favorite. Because you are choosing from multiple designs, there is no risk to you.

PeoplePerHour
(www.peopleperhour.com)

The main advantage of PeoplePerHour is the simple design of the site. It works like Fiverr, in the sense that freelancers can publish their projects at a fixed price, and Upwork, in which clients can publish works that freelancers can go through on their own. Another strong point of the site is that it supports a wide variety of categories.

PeoplePerHour provides the perfect balance between Fiverr and Upwork styles, making it an excellent choice for your outsourcing needs.

Behance (www.behance.net)

Behance is a premier outsourcing site, which means you'll find some of the best independent professionals on the web. This, however, means that you will spend more money on outsourcing.

High level outsourcing

Here are some of the benefits of using Behance:

✓ Using a powerful browser tab, you can find the world's most creative work based on field experience, tools and location.

✓ An updated activity source gives you access to a virtual control panel that tracks the creative work of your favorite freelancers.

✓ Freelancers can create beautiful portfolio pages that will show you your level of talent.

✓ A whole new experience for Followers with profile pages and curated collections.

While Behance is more expensive than most other outsourcing platforms, we guarantee you the best freelancers from all over the world.

CHAPTER IV
HIRING PROCESS

In your search for talent outsourcing, there are some crucial steps you should take that will help you to have an open mind regarding your ability to choose the right freelance for the nature of the job.

Create a clear job description

In order for you to determine exactly what you need in a self-employed worker, you must first list all the responsibilities necessary to successfully complete the job.

You need to be aware of the configuration of your business and where the self-employed will fit in. You should consider whether you will need a task-based freelancer, a full-time freelancer, or a part-time freelancer.

Depending on your business and your needs, you may need to hire several freelancers to perform micro-employment.

Once you have analyzed your needs, you will be able to create a clear job description that will allow potential candidates with the required skills and qualifications to apply for the job.

When writing the job description, include a keyword, requiring candidates to include it in the first line of their application, to ensure that they have read the job description in its entirety.

Detail job requirements

Many companies do not describe the specific job requirements because they simply want the project to be completed. They assume that the freelancer already has all the information about the job requirements. You need to determine precisely what resources are needed for the job to be successful.

This may be with respect to the necessary experience, Internet connections and skills, as well as personality traits. These are all the requirements you must determine to ensure a smooth flow of the business process you are outsourcing.

The description of the specific requirements will allow potential applicants to know if they are fit for the job. Taking this step will also provide you with guidance to narrow your selection and eventually hire the right independent worker who has the relevant experience and skills.

Determine how much you will pay

When you are looking to outsource your various business processes, you should know how much you are willing to spend on hiring an independent worker so you can budget how much you are going to spend on the job.

Before hiring a freelancer, you should talk to others who have worked successfully with freelancers to find out how much they usually pay for subcontracting. If you don't know anyone who has worked with self-employed workers before, you can research online to determine the average amount of money you must pay.

Self-Employment Assessment

Not all self-employed workers who apply for your job are qualified. You probably have a large group of interested candidates that you will have to evaluate before finding the best candidate for your job.

Examining each candidate's work history can be time-consuming. To help speed up this process, here's a simple system that will help you eliminate unqualified candidates quickly.

Take a quick look at all the applications and eliminate the ones that don't:

- Include the keyword
- Provide examples of similar projects
- Have a history of working on the site
- Have a feedback threshold of 4.0 or better
- Possess the specific skill set you need

Following this simple process will eliminate many candidates quickly, leaving you with the most qualified candidates.

Reducing your choice

After eliminating unqualified candidates, you will likely still have a large number of independent workers to choose from. Now you'll have to start looking more closely at the candidates and narrow your choices.

The goal is to identify 3 to 5 qualified freelancers for your subcontracted work. During this step, you will want to look carefully at the following criteria to help you narrow your search.

Offer Price - This is when you'll want to consider the budget you determined earlier in the process. Choose a range of acceptable bid prices, eliminating those above or below this number. Keep in mind that you get what you pay for; lower bids generally indicate that you will receive an inadequate level of service from the freelancer.

Companies v. Individuals - Take a look at the language used in the offer. If the candidate uses words like "we" or "our team," it is a good indication that he or she is representing a company.

Although you don't have to eliminate agencies automatically, you should carefully analyze your work history to determine if it's worth the increase in cost. If they do not provide exceptional service, they should be eliminated from consideration.

Customization - Many times you will

receive offers that include "cut and paste" responses that show that the candidate did not thoroughly read the job description. Although they may have included the keyword at the top of their application, they do so in a way that lacks any personal connection.

You want to look for candidates who are genuinely interested in the work you have published. They should include comments showing how they are uniquely qualified for the task.

Project Examples - See the job samples provided in each offer. It can be an image, an application, a website or a link to an article. Take a close look to see if they fit your needs and expectations.

Feedback ratings - For each candidate, click on the feedback ratings to see the work you have completed on the website. You may find that while some candidates have a high rate of feedback, they may not have any experience with your type of project. Eliminate any candidates with no related work experience.

Timeline - Time is money. Even the most qualified freelancers can waste your money if it takes forever to complete your project. Each offer you receive will include an expected timeline for completion. Pay attention to this date and eliminate offers that go beyond the norm.

Applying these simple rules can help you eliminate a large number of candidates. While you may have to repeat this step a couple of times, over time you may be able to narrow down the list of the most qualified candidates.

Choosing the Most Qualified Candidate

Now that you've narrowed your choices to a few highly qualified candidates, it's time to determine the best independent worker for the job. Here are five things you can do to help you make the final decision.

1) Create a small test

When it comes to successfully completing your project, punctuality and attention to detail are fundamental aspects of a successful project. You can "test" the handful of freelancers to determine if they have these qualities by providing them with a simple test to complete.

At this point, you can give each candidate a small task to see how quickly and accurately they complete it. Here are some ideas for testing your candidates.

- Ask them a question about your offer.
- Ask them to reaffirm their bid price.
- Ask them to sign a Confidentiality Agreement (NDA).
- Ask for another sample of their work.

The purpose here is to give each candidate a simple task that only takes a few minutes to complete.

Wait a day or so to see how each one responds. If someone gives you a lot of excuses or delays, it is a reliable indicator that you will get the same kind of service with your project.

2) Run a small project

If your project is complicated, you can pay a small fee to each qualified candidate and ask them to complete a small project. Give each one a similar task and see what comes to mind. You can ask them to design a simple application, create an icon or write an article. This is a great way to test candidates on their level of real experience.

3) Look for interest in the project

Take your time to examine each candidate's portfolio. You want to look for a personal interest in the market. Hire a candidate who is passionate about the type of project you offer to help you successfully complete the job. When someone has an interest in a market, they tend to work harder to do a good job.

4) Interviewing the candidate

You can use Skype (www.skype.com) to connect with people all over the world. It's a great tool for communicating and interviewing freelancers. You can do a phone interview, a video interview or a text interview with the tool's easy-to-use interface. If you don't feel comfortable using Skype, you can conduct the interview by email.

5) Check references

Most of the freelancers you work with will have references to previous work they have done. You should contact these former clients and talk to them about the candidate's previous job performance.

Ask about the quality of their work, their

punctuality, their communication skills, and their attitude toward the project. Don't be afraid to receive too many comments about each candidate.

Once you have completed these five steps, you should have narrowed your choice to the candidate who best fits the job. If you have a good feeling about one of the freelancers, then that's the person to hire.

CHAPTER V
AVOID A CATASTROPHE

Outsourcing your business tasks is not always an easy process. It can often turn into a stressful nightmare when it comes to a person who is not the right person for the job.

That's why it's crucial to follow these simple rules to avoid a subcontracting catastrophe.

Rule #1: Hire Slow

When you take the time to follow a long research process, you avoid many of the problems that arise from hiring low-quality freelancers. You can't just hire an individual based on their bid price and feedback. You have to take the time to challenge candidates from the beginning to make sure they are the right ones for the job.

Don't rush to choose the first qualified person to bid on your project. Instead, follow the five steps described above and take your time to find the perfect candidate.

Rule #2: Shoot Fast

Sometimes, no matter how much you research candidates, you will still end up hiring someone who is not fit for the job. The first thing to do in this case is to try to work with the self-employed. However, if they are continually making excuses or ignoring your corrections, then you need to get rid of them.

The best way to deal with poor freelancers is to get them out of your life quickly. You can use a "rule of three strikes" when firing a freelancer. When you get a third excuse or delay, immediately stop the project and try to recoup your investment.

The process of letting a self-employed person go can be complicated when it comes to money. It is crucial that you understand how disputes work on different outsourcing websites.

Rule #3: Avoid threatening them

The quickest way to worsen a stressful situation is to threaten a self-employed worker with negative feedback. Negative feedback can destroy a self-employed person's business, and you should never use it to get what you want. In reality, it should only be used when a self-employed worker possesses a poor character trait, such as lying or stealing.

Rule #4: Protect Your Ideas

There may be times when you want to protect an idea, this is especially true when outsourcing to a programmer for a mobile application or software. If you are concerned about people spying on your business, then you should have the freelancer sign a Confidentiality

Agreement.

Rule #5: Protect Your Confidential Information

When outsourcing to self-employed workers, you should also take appropriate precautions to protect your company's confidential information. You should be careful not to disclose any information that could harm your personal or professional life. While most freelancers are honest, revealing incorrect information can have disastrous consequences.

You want to make sure that you are only providing information to the self-employed worker that is directly related to the task at hand. Once the task is completed, be sure to change the password for those accounts. You should also be careful about giving away usernames and passwords that are similar to your PayPal account, bank account, and finances.

Most outsourcing projects you complete will do so without any problems. Use these rules as a guide to protect yourself from rare scenarios when something goes wrong.

Be sure to take your time with every new freelance you hire and use the tools provided by the various freelance sites, and you'll be able to overcome any problems that might arise if you hire an occasional lousy freelance.

CONCLUSION

Outsourcing is a great way to build a thriving business. It allows you to free up your time so you can focus on the crucial aspects of managing your business.

Outsourcing allows you to hire talented professionals who can complete projects that exceed the results you could achieve on your own.

When you surround yourself with talented professionals, you can delegate non-essential tasks and focus on critical functions that will help make your business successful.

Smart Outsourcing

Intelligent outsourcing is not about finding the least expensive freelance to complete the job. Instead, it's about being able to locate great talent and make it a virtual part of your day-to-day business operations.

Hiring others to take care of essential tasks can free up your time, allowing you to focus on the critical business activities that generate most of your profits.

Outsourcing can be one of the best moves you'll make for your business. All you have to do is analyze what you need and take the time to find the right candidate for the job and establish a strong working relationship with them.

Once you have achieved this, you can start concentrating on making your business stronger and more profitable. Just remember to protect yourself and your business

You will soon begin to realize that investing a small fraction of your money in hiring talented freelancers will pay off, giving your company higher profits and an outstanding reputation.

Remember that theory without practice is of no use to you, it takes to action everything you learn.

I wish you the best in your results.

A big hug, your friend Jorge!

By the way, I highly recommend you, if you want to learn how to cure work-related stress, my book, on "HOW TO HEAL THE CRONIC LABORAL STRESS EFFECTIVELY", is a book that I am sure will help you a lot in your path of "professional and business growth".

Without further ado, you can find it in the Amazon search engine, by title or by looking for my name, such as: "Jorge O. Chiesa". Once again, I wish you success in your results!

www.ingramcontent.com/pod-product-compliance
Lightning Source LLC
Chambersburg PA
CBHW072208170526
45158CB00004BB/1797